HE LOOKS LIKE ME

A Celebration of Lloyd Austin, our First African American Secretary of Defense

Lawanda D. Warthen
Illustrated by Taillefer Long

ISBN: 978-1-7366170-1-4
Library of Congress Control Number: 2021903526

Illustrations and Design by Taillefer Long,
IlluminatedStories.com

To the Austin family:

With Perseverance and Faith,
all things are possible!

Dreams do come true!

"Service to others is the rent we pay for our room in heaven."

–Muhammad Ali

A Message from the Author

This book is dedicated to my dear friend, Sonja Diane Foots, a nurse who served both in the military and then as a Department of Defense civilian. Before she lost her battle to cancer, Sonja, like General Lloyd Austin, lived an exemplary life serving others. And although she did not rise to the higher echelons of State power as General Austin did, she showed us that with love, courage, and fortitude, the least amongst us can become great in our own way. Sonja's greatness came from her heart of gold – her ability to make everyone she met feel better. Sonja left us way too soon, but her legacy lives on in her beautiful spirit and the example she set for us all.

My motivation in writing this book is to share with the world the story of a great soldier and hero, whose life and military contributions to the United States will become an important part of the US military's history for future generations. This is a story about the 28th Secretary of Defense, General Lloyd James Austin, III, a retired four-star general who served as the 12th Commander of United States Central Command (CENTCOM) and the 33rd Vice Chief of Staff of the US Army. General Austin is a superb role model for other Americans, both military and civilian, and his life serves as an outstanding example for future generations. His story represents the US Army as a melting pot of individuals from different races, backgrounds, and cultures, who are protecting our freedom. This book is important because it allows individuals who look like me to know they are not alone; with hard work and by doing the right thing they too are destined for greatness. I want to introduce the world to a great soldier and hero, a man of peace who proved to be an exemplary leader.

-Lawanda D. Warthen

He looks like me.

My name is Sonja and
I live in New Jersey.

This is my dog, Pumpkin.

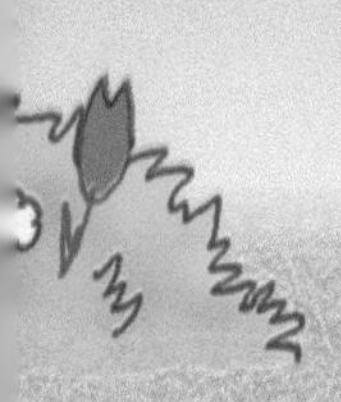

US
US
AUSTIN
AIRBORNE
RANGER

You can achieve greatness from humble beginnings

This is my hero.

He grew up in a small town in the South.

He served in the Army and became a general.

He looks like me.

Find good role models

When I look in the mirror
I see him.

Stay active in mind and body

He was close to his sisters,
who looked after him.
They enjoyed running,
playing, and reading.

I also enjoy these things.

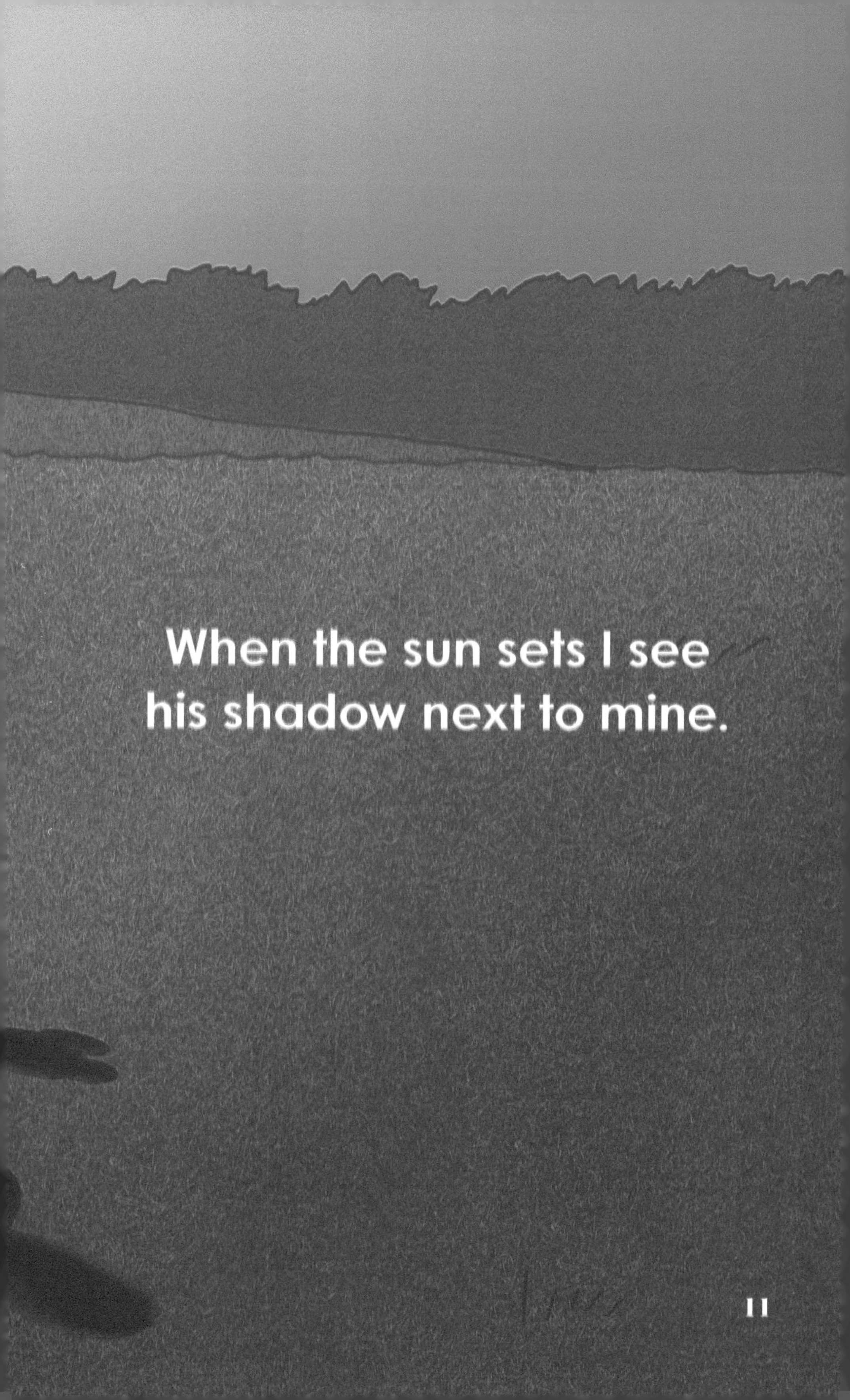

When the sun sets I see
his shadow next to mine.

I dream of being like him.

Believe in others
SONJA

He helps people.

Believe in God

He has faith.

Live by the golden rule

He treats everyone with dignity and respect.

Work hard, work together, and always aim high

He attended West Point.
He served in the military.

AUSTIN
AUSTIN
US ARMY

He embraced a number of adventures and went to many exciting places.

AUSTIN

One day I want to be in
the military like he was.
I want to achieve greatness.

Explore the world with an open mind

I too want to travel
to interesting places.

Serve a greater purpose

When he was in the military, he worked in the Pentagon and protected our freedoms around the world.

Believe in yourself

He is the first African
American Secretary
of Defense.

He shows me that I can
be and do anything.

I am proud because
I look like him.

About the Author

Lawanda Denise Warthen grew up in West Palm Beach, Florida. She is a graduate of Walden University, and holds a Doctorate in Healthcare Administration.

She resides in Woodbridge, Virginia, and works as the Director, Public Affairs, Army Medicine, Falls Church, Virginia. She enjoys reading and traveling with family and friends.

Lightning Source UK Ltd.
Milton Keynes UK
UKHW050658160821
388842UK00001B/11
9781736617014